Your Health Is Your Next Generation's Wealth

Ademola O. Adeyeni

Your Health Is Your Next Generation's Wealth

Cover design by: Karen Warner

Published by: K. Warner

Good health gives us time on this earth to generate as much wealth as possible. If everyone had enough time, we would eventually all be wealthy. The problem is we run out of time to accomplish a lot of things that we want to do in life. A lot of it has to do with how much finances we have at the start of our journey. Having access to tangible and intangible assets allows us to accomplish things in our lifetime at a faster pace. For some of us, we do not have the luxury of good health and therefore have less time. This is when it is time to pass the baton to the next generation, for them to carry the torch and continue our legacy.

Ninety-five percent of the world's population has health problems and should therefore not have any difficulty understanding the depth of this title. The term “health is wealth” takes on a whole new meaning. My grandparents were born in the early 1900s and were poor by today's standards. They did not have the basics that most take for granted. They did not have running water, electricity or modern cooking appliances or access to basic modern medicine. They did not own a vehicle. Their purchasing power put them in the poverty bracket. Back in those days in my Nigerian culture, it was customary and acceptable for a man to have multiple wives. Both of my grandfathers had multiple wives and had many children. My grandfather on my father's side owned farmland and enlisted the help of his wives and children to till the land daily. His wives sold the crops at the market to support the family. They did not get a western education. The assets that they were able to pass on to their children were acres of farmland and a six-bedroom house.

My dad has been renting his inherited one-bedroom portion out to someone for decades. His inherited portion of land is being farmed by family members. My grandparents, from my mom's side, were a little different. My mom's father also had multiple wives but he had a high school education and a two year post high school degree. He had a career as a teacher. My grandmother on my mom's side did not receive a western education. She owned and ran a retail shop.

My grandparents toiled and worked very hard and made enough money to give my mom and my dad a basic western high school education. My dad wanted to further his education by enrolling into nursing school in the 60s but neither he nor his parents had the money to pay for the education. A Nursing Career in the late 50s and early 60s in Nigeria was very lucrative. British Catholic Westerners established a Nursing school program in their town at the time. It was the only Nursing program in a 500-mile radius. They had a strict selective guideline process that initially disqualified my dad. One of the disqualifying items for my dad was that a candidate was required to be of Catholic Faith and also that the tuition must be paid in full. My Dad was a Christian and not Catholic. He did not have the financial resources or connections to get into the program he so desired. He begged his mom and dad for the money to pay for the program because there was only one more slot left in the program to a candidate that met the guideline. He explained to them how important getting into this program will be in changing the course of his financial future. My dad had observed for years how a select few from the students who graduated from this institution have had life changing careers. He saw their financial lives radically transform from living meagerly to being prosperous. Nurses during those times were almost as equal to General

Practitioner Doctors in terms of status and academics. My dad relentlessly pleaded with his mom to help him with the money. She had no money at all. She sold trinkets and small items to survive. By this time, his parents had been divorced for years. She saw how desperate her only son sounded when he pleaded for help with the tuition. Her compassion and deep love for her son inspired her to relentlessly find anyone who will lend her the money. She eventually found someone to borrow the money from. At the same time he was asking her for tuition help, my dad was looking for ways to come up with the money. He had been purposefully attending their Sunday catholic services and eventually joined the Catholic Church. He graduated nursing school in the mid 60s and gained enough practical skills and experience and was inspired to open two Nursing Clinics of his own, years later.

My parents migrated to the US in the late 60s and my dad attained his master's degree in health care administration and my mom got her Associates Degree. My grandparents' good health allowed them to utilize their hands and feet to toil their farmland, become a teacher and sell items for decades. The decades of hard work with little to no education gave them a life with no luxuries. They were only able to afford food, shelter and a few clothes. I was told that they built their houses themselves. Everything required manual hard labor in my grandparent's era. They lived in mud houses, no electricity, and no running water. Because their good health allowed them to have the basics, it laid a foundation for my dad and my mom to benefit from their decades of spent labor. Their decades of spent labor produced tangible assets and intangible assets which is real estate and acres of farmland and limited western education for their children. My parents are healthy and are in their golden years now. They are retired and have done well for themselves. My dad retired as a Registered Nurse a decade ago. My mom also retired as a Nurses Aid seven years ago. They have multiple real estate properties in the States and abroad. They are not lacking in anything. They live in a modest house in NYC that they own and can afford to have running water, 24-hour electricity and do not suffer the hardships of poverty like their parents did. My parents were blessed with three children. Through their knowledge and vision of generational wealth, they made sure we were set up with a debt free education.

My siblings and I are fortunate enough to receive a western education. As we started our careers with no debt, it gave us the proper foundation for building wealth quickly. All of us have a genetic disease called Sickle Cell Anemia, which is a blood disorder that can cause many life-threatening problems. To put it in perspective for every reader, Sickle Cell pain crisis is worse than childbirth pain and just as bad as cancer pain; according to the NIH, (National Institute of Health).

My quality of life is not great due to my health challenges. I have health limitations that interrupt the process of generational wealth to a degree. My inability to progress in a career is linked to my health. The mental anguish and the shame that I have is immeasurable. I am constantly comparing myself to my mom and dad's accomplishments in successfully achieving a lengthy consistent employment history before they retired. I know I should not compare myself to them, but they have always been my measuring stick. An education and a successful career have always been my parents' expectations for me. I find myself comparing myself to my peers as well. It has been extremely hard for me to model my path after someone with good health because I always find myself falling short due to my frequent episodes. However, I have found ways to give my life meaning and contribute to my next generation's success story. My physical limitations forced me to use my brain to figure out ways to succeed financially. After years of self education in the crypto currency space, I was able to recognize the future success of this space. For people who are close to me, I tried to confer with them about it, but they dismissed the technology and stated that it was not going to go anywhere. I was now faced with the choice of whether I was going to follow what they said or listen to my intuition. I chose to follow my intuition. I felt alone during my journey but because I had spent many months and years educating myself, it was an easy decision for me. A few years later, the decision I made paid off. The crypto currency market took off and gave me the ability to afford and buy our new house. I encourage my reader to be open to novel and new ideas.

As a father of two teenage daughters, I recently realized that I am doing something right. They are developing good money habits and have a good head on their shoulders. They are determined and understand the concept of budgeting and know the difference between needs and wants in their lives. They have mastered the art of arresting the emotional urge of instant gratification. I am so proud of them and am confident that they are going to be successful with just these skills. My 19-year-old already has a 761-credit score. We will find out what my 17-year-old daughter's score is when she turns 18 next year. My daughter's high credit score was intentionally planed approximately three years ago. I added both of them as users on my credit card and bank account since they were 15 years old. My 19-year-old opened her own bank account when she turned 18. My 17-year-old is still a minor and still on my credit card and on my bank account as a separate user. If my 19-year-old wants to take out a loan from the bank or buy a new car with her good credit today, she will be offered the best favorable interest rate. I have taught them to hate bad debt.

Speed and time are irrelevant when you are thinking two generations ahead. My employment history has been inconsistent, and I am still not financially content. My journey continues on the road to accumulate as much tangible and intangible assets as possible to leave for my next generation. I am feeling optimistic about my role in the lineage history of the next two generations.

Take very good care of your body and your mind because how you treat yourself can determine the course of your future generations. Do everything in moderation. Do not overindulge. Exercise your body, mind and spirit daily. Your impact on your future generations can be measured in one or two generations if you plan and execute your moves at the right time at and at the right place. What you do today will matter in their lives tomorrow. Generational wealth is real and can be achieved in a generation. You must be intentional in your direction in life. Plan and execute. Do not be anxious and inpatient about your future. If you can reprogram your mind and believe that toiling today will benefit your next generation, you will start to do everything in your life with purpose. We tend to always focus on ourselves and what we want today. Looking ahead and planning is a challenge most of us face. If you start thinking two generations ahead, it will put things into perspective; that is your grandchildren's future. Take a moment and meditate on this thought for a minute. Ask yourself and visualize what type of environment they are living in. Visualize the type of opportunity and legacy you want to leave for them. Did you leave them assets or opportunities that will serve as a foundation that they can build on? Are they suffering because of the unwise decisions you or your parents made?

Most of us are on a journey to find ourselves and find a career that gives us meaning. Very few have opportunities created by their parents and grandparents. Most are beginning from nothing and will be the first to lay the foundation for future generational wealth through hard work. Let's look at a few notable people or families who poured the first foundation for generational wealth:

Bill and Dave started Hewlett Packard from the garage of the house they bought together on January 1, 1939. Their mission in starting HP was to contribute to society through the products they build. HP still exists to this day and continues to build on the foundation it laid from its inception of arduous work. They are now worth 34.70 billion dollars (about $110 per person in the US).

Another person or company who laid the first foundation for generational wealth is Henry Ford with Ford Motor Company. He built his first experimental car in a workshop behind his home in 1896. Henrys hard work and dedication did not come without challenges and setbacks. With a determination to succeed, he conquered all obstacles. The Ford family still owns an equity stake and voting power in the company today. Their annual revenue is 136.3 billion. Opportunities will occasionally present themselves in your lifetime that if taken, it will define the course of your future. If my dad had not taken the once in a lifetime opportunity to get into that nursing program at that moment in time, who knows where else my dad would have ended up, and who knows if he would have turned out as successful as he did. Many of his colleagues that he went to school with never had the opportunity to get into the nursing school which earned him a good wage; allowed him to establish a business and opened doors to travel abroad.

A few moments in time, opportunities come to all of us. The secret to capturing and responding to those moments is to *ALWAYS OBEY YOUR INTUITION*. We all have that gut feeling, inner voice, inner spirit that strongly warns us of impending danger and shows us opportunities to take. I have made many mistakes in my past because I dismissed my intuition. Five years ago, I reflected on my life and realized that all the bad judgments I have made in my life were because I ignored my inner voice. That is one thing I have decided to change in my life, which has so far been serving me well. I do not know what it will be for you, but you must recognize the power of your intuition. We are not trained or taught to focus on this part of our being. There is a huge disconnect in our society about our intuition. Our intuition will never steer us wrong or allow us to make a bad decision. It is pure and unbiased. It doesn't have any political views and it does not discriminate. Its only purpose is to protect you, guide you and affirm your decisions. It is important to learn this aspect of yourself as early as possible to prevent making avoidable mistakes that can set you back months, years, or even decades of your life.

I would like to remind you and stress the things that I believe are important for your future and generational wealth success:

1) Always be intentional every day in everything you do.

2) Have a vision board.

3) Write out your short-term goals and long-term goals.

4) Always take the long view perspective in every decision you make.

5) Meditate as often as possible to learn how to easily recognize when your inner voice is speaking to you.

6) Be patient. With time all your goals will fall into place, even if it takes a generation. Your legacy will thank you and remember you for your sacrifice. Your greatest gift is health and time.

7) Obey your intuition, it will save you.

8) Keep your body and mind healthy.

This is the life cycle of generational wealth:

1. Health – Good health

2. Spent Labor – Performed physical tasks

3. Currency – Money earned

4. Assets – Tangible and intangible things that increases in value over time

5. Income (Residual) – Income resulting from selling assets or assets that produces residual income. For example: Perpetual rental income, etc.

~~~
~~~

Thank you for taking the time to read this book. I hope by reading this book you have developed a new perspective on how to navigate your future. Please share your newfound knowledge with your friends and family. I wish you the best of luck on your journey into the future.

Dedication

This book is dedicated to my daughters, Sade' and Kemi.

Your existence gives me a reason to keep striving.

Daddy will always love you!

Karen, my love, you are the most sweetest and kind hearted person in my life. Thank for you for always being honest

with me. I love you.